TEACH YOURSELF

Bluegrass Banjo

by Tony Trischka

Teach yourself authentic bluegrass. Clear instructions from a professional; basics,
right- and left-hand techniques, solos, backup, personal advice on performance and much more.
Plus a complete selection of the best bluegrass songs and tunes to learn from.

Cover photography of banjo by Randall Wallace
Background cover photography by Herb Wise
Project editors: Peter Pickow and Ed Lozano
Musical contractor: Bob Grant
Interior design and layout: Don Giller

This book Copyright © 1979 by Amsco Publications,
A Division of Music Sales Corporation, New York
This edition published 1999 by Oak Publications,
A Division of Embassy Music Corporation, New York

PLAYBACK+
Speed • Pitch • Balance • Loop

To access audio visit:
www.halleonard.com/mylibrary

Enter Code
3656-6603-7206-2425

ISBN 978-0-8256-0323-5

For all works contained herein:
Unauthorized copying, arranging, adapting, recording, internet posting, public performance,
or other distribution of the music in this publication is an infringement of copyright.
Infringers are liable under the law.

Visit Hal Leonard Online at
www.halleonard.com

Contact us:
Hal Leonard
7777 West Bluemound Road
Milwaukee, WI 53213
Email: info@halleonard.com

In Europe, contact:
Hal Leonard Europe Limited
42 Wigmore Street
Marylebone, London, W1U 2RN
Email: info@halleonardeurope.com

In Australia, contact:
Hal Leonard Australia Pty. Ltd.
4 Lentara Court
Cheltenham, Victoria, 3192 Australia
Email: info@halleonard.com.au

Audio Track Listing

Audio Personnel

Tony Trischka: Banjo

Bob Grant: Mandolin, Guitar, and Vocals

Antoine Silverman: Fiddle

Matt Weiner: Bass

Table of Contents

Introduction

Right now the five-string banjo is experiencing a greater popularity than at any other time in its history. Thanks to *Dueling Banjos* (from *Deliverance*), *Foggy Mountain Breakdown* (from *Bonnie and Clyde*), and a flood of commercials that feature five-string, banjo mania is reaching epic proportions. At the heart of all this excitement is a smooth, driving style that has the power to dramatically vary the texture of a bluegrass band. Rippling gently at first during the backup, the banjo can suddenly explode into a torrent of notes on the lead break and then quietly recede once more into the background. This book will show you how to get these sounds and use them effectively in a band context.

You'll start with the absolute basics: tunings, chords, etc. Then you'll move step-by-step through the three major bluegrass styles: Scruggs—the essential three-finger approach named after its developer, Earl Scruggs; Reno—a hot swing style created by Don Reno, a contemporary of Earl's; and melodic—the fiddle tune style popularized by Bill Keith in the early 60s. From there you'll turn to sections on backup, tunings, and improvisation. In addition, there will be some twenty-five songs, many of them bluegrass standards, arranged with the basic melody on one line and the lead break just below it. This will make it easier for you to learn the unfamiliar songs and will also show you how the bluegrass style embellishes a melody.

One more fringe benefit: there are three other books in this series, covering the guitar, fiddle, and mandolin. Since they have a number of songs in common with this book, you might consider getting together with a guitar player who has the guitar book, or a fiddle player who has the fiddle book, and begin trading licks. Of course, you'll have to learn how to play first, so let's get started.

In the Beginning

Tuning

Before we begin, let's pause for a moment and make sure you're in tune. The easiest way to do this is by tuning to a piano in the following manner:

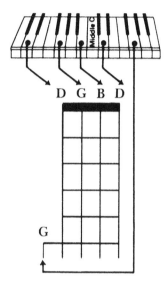

If you find your notes are a little above (or sharp to) those of the piano, just tune down carefully until you reach the desired note. Likewise, if you're below (or flat), tune up.

Now you may not always have access to a piano, so pick up a pitch pipe at your local music store. Tune your third string to the G note of the pipe and then use this method to get the rest of your banjo in tune:

Match the fifth fret of the fourth string with the open string (G).

Match the fourth fret of the third string with the open second string (B).

Match the third fret of the second string with the open first string (D).

Match the fifth fret of the first string with the open fifth string (G).

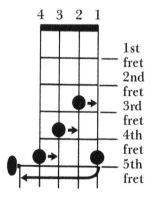

In instances where you're playing with other people, you can always tune to them. Have them play a G, D, or B note, get in sync with that and tune the rest of your banjo in the way I described above.

Left Hand Position

A correct left-hand position is crucial if you ever hope to play with speed and accuracy.

Start by holding the banjo neck in the crook of your hand (between the thumb and index fingers). Now, without worrying about which strings you're pushing down, place your fingers firmly on the fretboard.

As you do this make sure your hand is relaxed. If it is, you'll have a much easier time moving fluidly from position to position.

Another way to increase your speed and mobility is by keeping your fingers poised within close striking range of the strings. The shorter the distance between your fingers and the strings the faster you'll be able to fret the notes you want. When you are actually pressing down on the strings, your fingers should hug closely to the next highest fret.

This will help you avoid string buzz, one of the main obstacles standing between you and a good clean sound. You should also be sure you're not accidentally fretting two strings at the same time. For instance, in using your index finger to push down the third string at the second fret, you may discover part of your fingertip or nail damping the fourth string at the same fret. If this is a chronic problem for you, just keep your awareness focused on your fingers until the sloppy fretting clears up.

Once you have these points fixed in your mind, you can move on to the next section.

Chords

If you've done much listening to bluegrass, country and western or primal rock and roll you may have noticed that many of the tunes contain only three chords. These are known as I, IV, and V chords. So that you understand the meaning of these numbers, I'd like to talk about scales for a moment.

If you learned your do-re-mi's in elementary school, you'll recall that there are eight notes in a scale: do, re, mi, fa, sol, la, ti, and do. Since the I, IV and V refer to the chords based on the first, fourth and fifth notes in a scale, we're talking about do, fa, and sol.

The I (do), IV (fa) and V (sol) chords we'll be using most often here are found in the key of G: G, C and D.

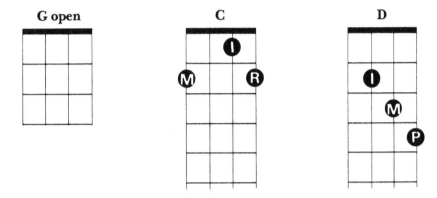

In C they turn out to be C, F and G.

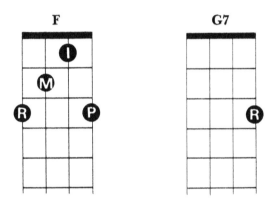

This next diagram lists the I, IV and V chords for the seven major keys.

Keys	I	IV	V
A	A	D	E
B	B	E	F♯
C	C	F	G
D	D	G	A
E	E	A	B
F	F	B♭	C
G	G	C	D

If you're playing a song in the key of G, but your lead singer has to cross his or her legs to hit the high note, you may want to switch to a more comfortable key. This is known as transposing. To make transposing fun and easy, simply consult the chart to find the I, IV and V chords in your new home key.

With the addition of this next set of chords, you'll be able to transpose into any of the seven major keys.

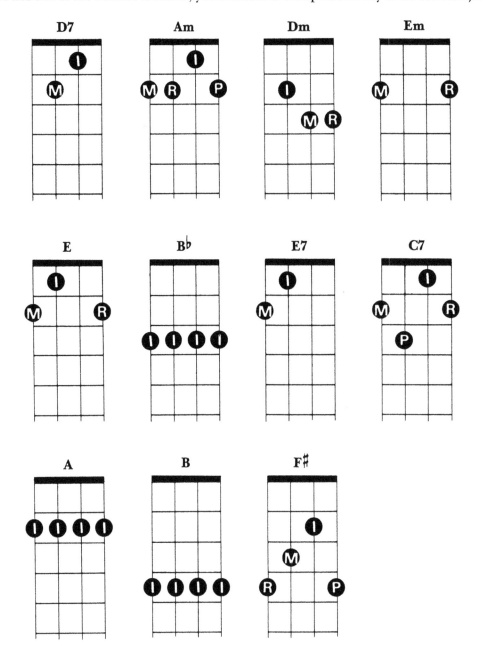

You won't need all these chords for this book, but I've included them here in case you decide to go progressive at some point in the future.

Now that you're ready to start playing, strum through *Red River Valley* and *Amazing Grace,* substituting the chords of your choice for the I, IV and V designations. For starters, stick to the keys of G, C and D. These are the ones you'll be playing most often in the pages ahead. In case you're wondering about the hieroglyphics under the words, the dark strokes represent down-beats (when your foot is tapping the floor in time with the music) and the light strokes represent up-beats (the in-between points when your foot is raised off the floor).

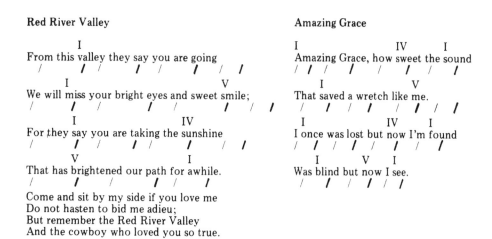

Red River Valley

       I
From this valley they say you are going
/ / /   /   /   /   /

       I   V
We will miss your bright eyes and sweet smile;
/   /   /   /   /   /   /

       I   IV
For they say you are taking the sunshine
/   /   /   / /   /   /

    V   I
That has brightened our path for awhile.
/   /   /   / /   /

Come and sit by my side if you love me
Do not hasten to bid me adieu;
But remember the Red River Valley
And the cowboy who loved you so true.

Amazing Grace

I   IV   I
Amazing Grace, how sweet the sound
/ /   /   /   /   /   /

I   V
That saved a wretch like me.
/   /   /   /   /   / /   /

I   IV   I
I once was lost but now I'm found
/   /   /   /   /   /   /

     I   V   I
Was blind but now I see.
/   /   / /   /

The important thing to remember here, as in the rest of the book, is to take it slowly at first. Get every note clean and even. Concentrate on keeping a steady rhythm (I recommend working with a metronome). Then when you have everything under control, start picking up the tempo. This is the only way to get good results from your practicing.

Inversions

An inversion is simply another way of fingering a particular chord somewhere else on the neck. For instance, you can find your basic G chord by strumming the open strings:

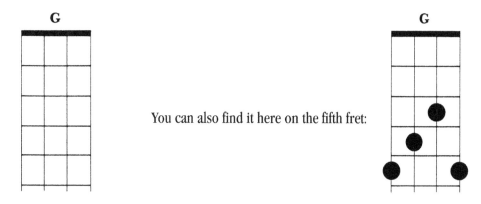

You can also find it here on the fifth fret:

Notice that the second inversion is the basic F position moved up two frets. To get a better understanding of how this works, familiarize yourself with the notes on the piano keyboard.

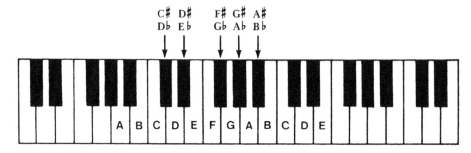

By going from one piano key to the very next one, black or white, or from one banjo fret to the next consecutive one, you'll be moving one half step. This is known as moving chromatically. So, to go back to our inversions, there are two half steps between F and G—from F to F♯ and from F♯ to G. Thus if you want to play a second inversion G chord, simply take your F and move it up two frets.

To get the next G inversion, look at your basic D chord. By checking the keyboard you can see that there are five half steps between D and G. So just move your D position up five frets and you'll have a ninth fret G.

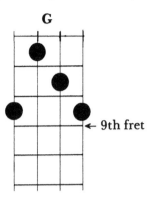

G

← 9th fret

With this knowledge, you'll be able to find the different inversions for any chord.

The Capo

The capo is a convenient device that allows you to play in different keys without changing basic left-hand positions. Since bluegrass is most comfortably played on the banjo in the G, C, and D positions, those are the ones you're going to want to stay with. So if your lead singer insists on singing in the key of B, you can simply clamp your capo on the fourth fret (B is four half steps above G) and continue to play out of the hard driving open G position.

Don't forget, you also have to capo your fifth string the same number of frets as the other four strings. There are fifth string capos available that attach to the side of your banjo neck. However, I recommend model railroad tracks hammered into the seventh, ninth and tenth frets.

Make sure you have this done by a competent repair person to avoid the woodpecker look on your neck.

Tablature and Timing

All the tunes in this book are written out in tablature. This is a simple system of notation that relates specifically to the instrument for which it is written. For instance, we'll be using a five line staff—one line for each string of the banjo.

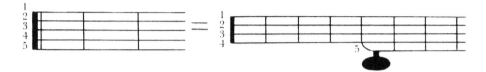

The vertical lines intersecting the staff above are called barlines. They divide the staff into measures. Each measure in a particular tune will have the same time value, be it $\frac{2}{4}$, $\frac{3}{4}$, $\frac{4}{4}$, or whatever. Now let me explain what this means. Most of the tunes you'll be playing will be in $\frac{4}{4}$ time: in other words, there will be four quarter notes per measure.

As I mentioned in the chord section, the dark strokes are the beats and the light strokes are the off-beats.
You can divide those quarter notes into smaller units called eighth notes. Eight eighth notes = four quarter notes.

This is the configuration you'll come across most often in this book.

Occasionally, we'll be dealing with sixteenth notes. Sixteen sixteenth notes = eight eighth notes, etc. Whereas eighth notes are connected by a single line (or beam), sixteenth notes are branded with a double line.

The final note we'll be dealing with is the half note. The half note is the equivalent of two quarter notes and will be indicated here simply by a number with no stem and no beams.

By now your mind is probably swimming with all of this new information. But stick with it. After a few songs you'll get the feel for it.

From time to time you'll see two notes connected with a loop (or tie).

This indicates that you should pick only the first note but allow it to ring for the time value of both (in this case two beats).

Here's an example that will get you more in touch with counting time.

So far this has all sounded suspiciously like standard musical notation. But here's the difference. Instead of actual music, notes will be indicated in terms of numbers. These numbers represent the fret on the fingerboard that the left hand is to play. For instance:

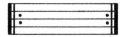

This means you'll pick the third fret of the third string. Other indications: a zero (0) represents an open string and an X on the third string represents a sixteenth note rest (or space where no note is played). Directly underneath the numbers will be the right-hand fingerings, designated thusly:

T = thumb

1 = index finger

2 = middle finger

Here's an example:

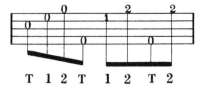

There are a few other indications with which you'll come in contact later, but for now this is all you'll need.

One other symbol you'll need to know is the repeat sign. This designation will be used when an entire section of apiece (part A or part B) is to be repeated. That section will be enclosed within these two signs:

Sometimes the section will have two endings, indicated like this:

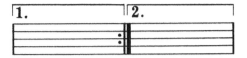

When you see this, start at the beginning of the section and play through the first ending. Then go back to the beginning of the same section and play it again, this time skipping the first ending and playing the second.

Finally, a word about the general format of the music. Each song will be laid out in groups of two connected staves. The top staff will feature the melody, and the bottom staff features the lead break that is based on that melody. When there are lyrics, they'll appear between the connected staves. In cases where the melody line is sparsely noted, no right hand fingerings will be indicated.

Now that we've established the ground rules, let's get started.

Scruggs Style

If it hadn't been for Earl Scruggs, old Mastertones would probably be selling in pawn shop windows today for $200 instead of $800. Indeed, Earl is the recognized father and popularizer of the three-finger bluegrass style of banjo playing and as such is responsible for the banjo mania rampant today. He rose to prominence under the wing of another father—the father of bluegrass, Bill Monroe. That was in 1945. A few years later, Earl and a young guitar player named Lester Flatt branched off to form their own band, the Foggy Mountain Boys. By the 1960s Flatt and Scruggs had become a household word, thanks to their *Theme from Bonnie and Clyde (Foggy Mountain Breakdown)* and the *Ballad of Jed Clampett.*

Today Scruggs style serves as the foundation for all bluegrass banjo playing. It has a way of driving a band like mad and in so doing creates enough excitement to knock the average listener's socks in the creek. Let's start with the basics.

Fingerpicks

When a bluegrass band kicks into overdrive it may not be able to compete decibel for decibel with Led Zeppelin, but it can put out enough sound to draw a rush hour crowd in Times Square. To make sure you can reach those sound levels when you need to, you're going to want fingerpicks on your right hand. The effect of metal (picks) on metal (strings) will give you more volume than you could ever get with your bare fingers.

As you can see, the fingerpicks should be placed on the index and middle fingers so that the hook-like extension covers the bottom of your fingertip. Make sure the picks are on snugly, but not to the degree that they cut off the circulation to your fingertips. Once you have these firmly in place, add either a plastic or metal thumbpick to your thumb. Now these picks may feel awkward at first but stick with them. They'll give you that loud, crisp tone so desirable for bluegrass playing.

Right Hand Position

There are a number of different ways to position your right hand for bluegrass playing, but this one is probably the most common: Plant your pinky and ring finger on the head of the banjo, approximately half an inch in front of the bridge and half an inch from the stings. This support will allow you to pick with as much drive and speed as you need. However, if your tendons won't cooperate and you find it impossible to keep both fingers down, opt for the one finger that feels most comfortable.

Once you've made your choice of fingers (or finger) you can vary their distance from the bridge slightly to produce the exact sound you want to hear from your instrument. The closer you are the harsher the tone will be; the farther away, the more mellow.

Now, arch your hand at the wrist so that you have a strong downward attack on the strings. Experiment here also to find the position that's most comfortable for you.

Licks and Rolls

The basis for Scruggs style is actually quite simple—the roll. A roll refers to three or four notes played in various combinations by the right hand. Try these on for size:

the forward roll:

T 1 2

the backward roll:

2 1 T

forward backward roll:

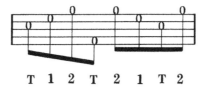

T 1 2 T 2 1 T 2

thumb one thumb two (T1T2):

T 1 T 2

With these four rolls you can actually do quite a lot. I've interspersed them liberally in this next version of *Bile 'Em Cabbage Down* to give you a taste of what you'll be playing in the rest of the book.

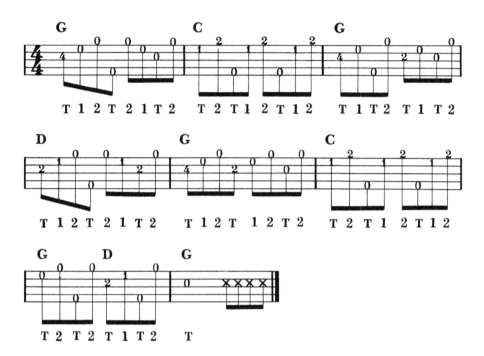

Now this is fine, but you're still not playing Scruggs style. Missing are the characteristic licks that make a banjo solo instantly identifiable as bluegrass. However, if we take the right-hand rolls you already know and combine them with a few new left-hand techniques, you'll suddenly find your playing transformed into Scruggs style.

Let's start with the slide. Place the middle finger of your right hand on the second fret of the third string and slide it up just past the third fret. Make sure you emphasize the second fret note before you start sliding. Here's how that looks in tablature.

Scruggs gets basically the same sound by sliding from the second to the third fret, so choose the one that feels most comfortable to you. Now let's put the slide together with a forward roll.

As you can see, the second string should be picked as you reach the top of the slide. Also be aware of your timing. For now, each note should be played with the same emphasis and time value as every other.

We can get a variation on the above lick by combining the slide with a T1T2 roll.

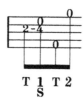

Now let's put these two slide licks into context with this second version of *Bile 'Em Cabbage Down.*

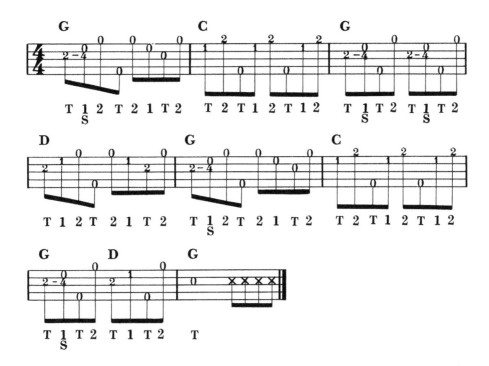

Here's another slide, based on the fourth string, which crops up a lot in bluegrass.

This can also be integrated into either a forward roll:

of a T1T2 roll:

Next we have the pull-off. Although this requires a little more finesse to play correctly, you should have no problem mastering it. Place the middle finger of your left hand on the second fret of the first string. Now, just pull off in a downward direction so that you hear the open first string. Remember, don't just lift your finger off. Be aggressive and pull down on the string. You shouldn't even have to pick with the right hand at all to hear the open first string.

Let's create another context for the pull-off. As well as pulling-off to an open string, you can pull-off to a fretted string. Using your middle finger again, place it on the third fret of the third string and this time push off in the direction of the fourth string.

Simultaneously, place your index finger on the second fret of the third string. By doing this you should be able to hear first the third fret note and then the second fret note. Remember, the idea is to get two notes by picking one. Here's that pull-off (or push-off, if you will) in tablature.

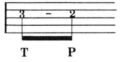

If you find your middle finger brushing against the fourth string, don't worry. When it's put in the context of a song, that sound will be lost in the avalanche of other notes. Now let's combine this pull-off with a T1T2 roll to get a very popular Scruggs lick that you'll find in *Cripple Creek, Roll in My Sweet Baby's Arms* and countless other tunes.

Notice the extra beam connecting the 3 and the 2. This indicates that the 3 and 2 are both sixteenth notes and should be played twice as fast as the other three notes that are eighth notes. TO make the timing of this clearer, here's the same lick with down-beats and up-beats indicated.

From here we can move to the hammer-on. This is a very simple technique that involves picking a string and then plunking down a finger of the left hand on a higher fret of the same string. Try these hammer-ons.

The first two are played by placing the index finger of your left hand on the second fret and then hammering-on to the third with the middle finger. The last hammer-on involves picking the open fourth string and then hammering-on to the second fret with the middle finger of the left hand.

These hammer-ons can also be combined with various right-hand rolls to create three common Scruggs licks.

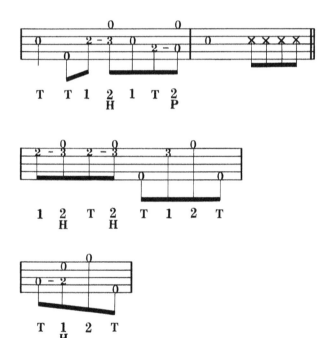

At this point you're ready to tackle a couple of full-fledged songs—*Cripple Creek* and *Red River Valley*. If you have any trouble with them, just go back to the section on tablature or this section, depending on where your trouble lies. Remember: don't forge ahead until you understand everything you've already covered. Enjoy.

Red River Valley

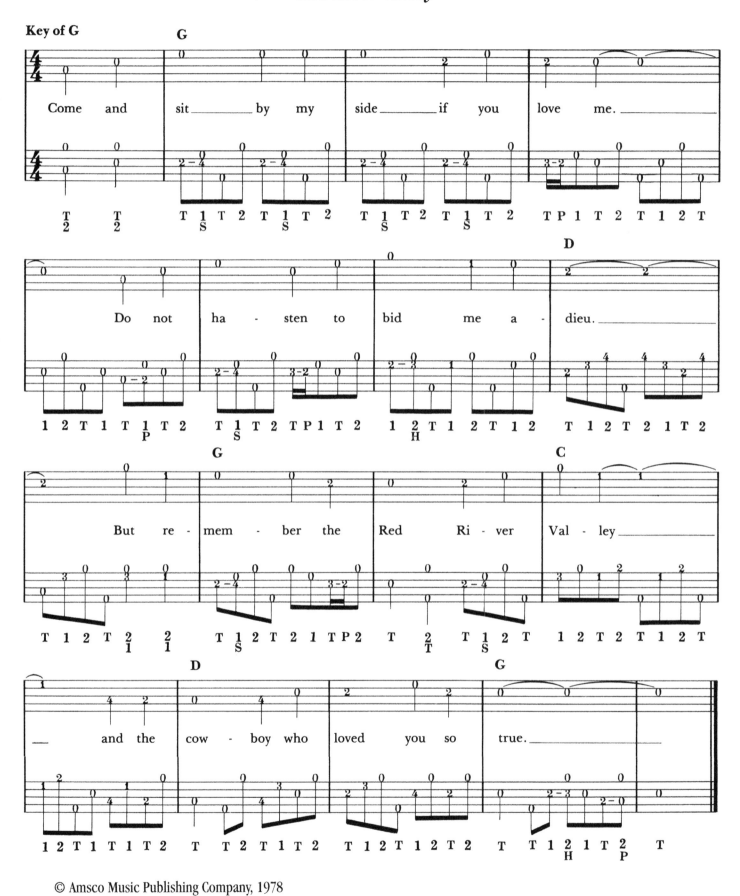

Cripple Creek

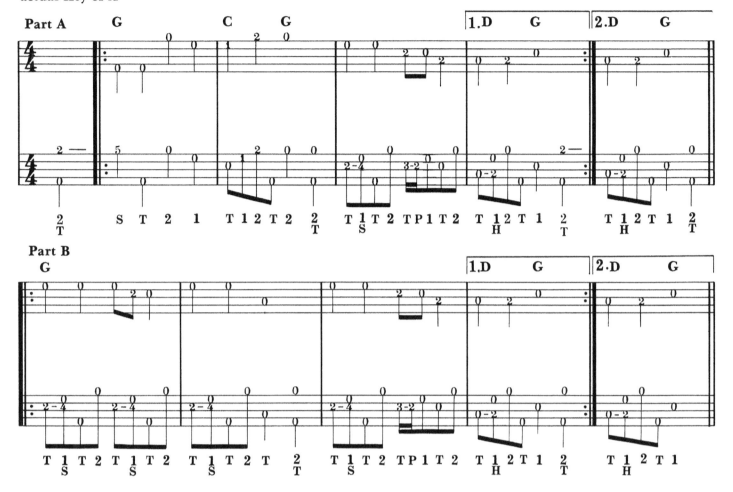

Before I let you loose on the rest of the tunes in this section, there are two more techniques I want to cover—choking and harmonics.

Choking

To choke, fret one of the strings and then push up on it so that you're actually bending the string. As well as being a good release for your aggressions, this is the best way to get a bluesy sound out of your instrument.

In bluegrass, the tenth fret of the second string is an excellent locale for a choke. Try this lick. (An arrow over a note indicates a choke.)

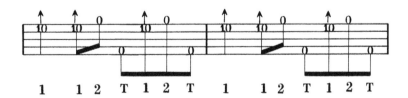

Harmonics

Harmonics are the closest the banjo comes to sounding like the heavenly bells. In fact this technique is sometimes known as chiming the strings. To get this sound, place the index finger of your left hand very lightly over the first four strings, directly on top of the twelfth fret. Now pick.

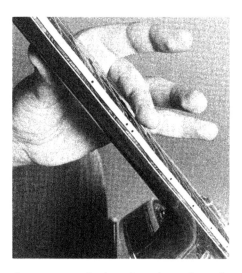

This will give you a supernal G chord, one octave higher than the unfretted open G tuning. You can also find a G harmonic at the fifth fret and a D harmonic at the seventh fret. Other more obscure harmonics are hidden elsewhere on the neck.

There are two good examples of harmonics in this book—the beginning of *Bugle Call Rag* and the ending to the backup for *All the Good Times.* You'll be able to locate the harmonics by looking for the little H placed just to the right of the note.

Music maestro, please—

Old Joe Clark

Roll in My Sweet Baby's Arms

Capo on 2nd fret:
actual Key of A

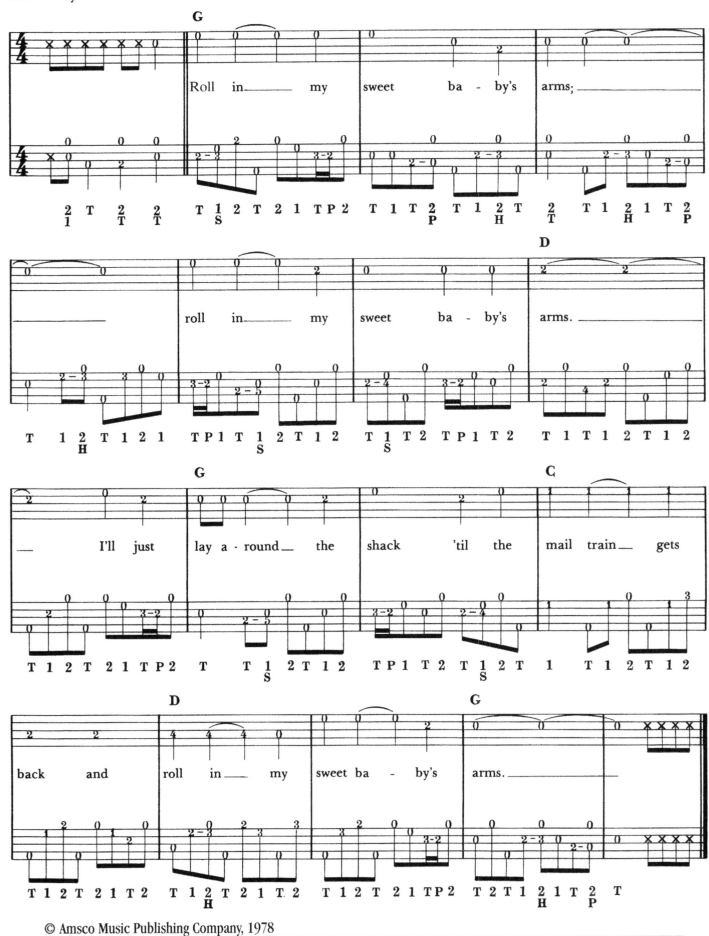

Little Maggie

Key of G

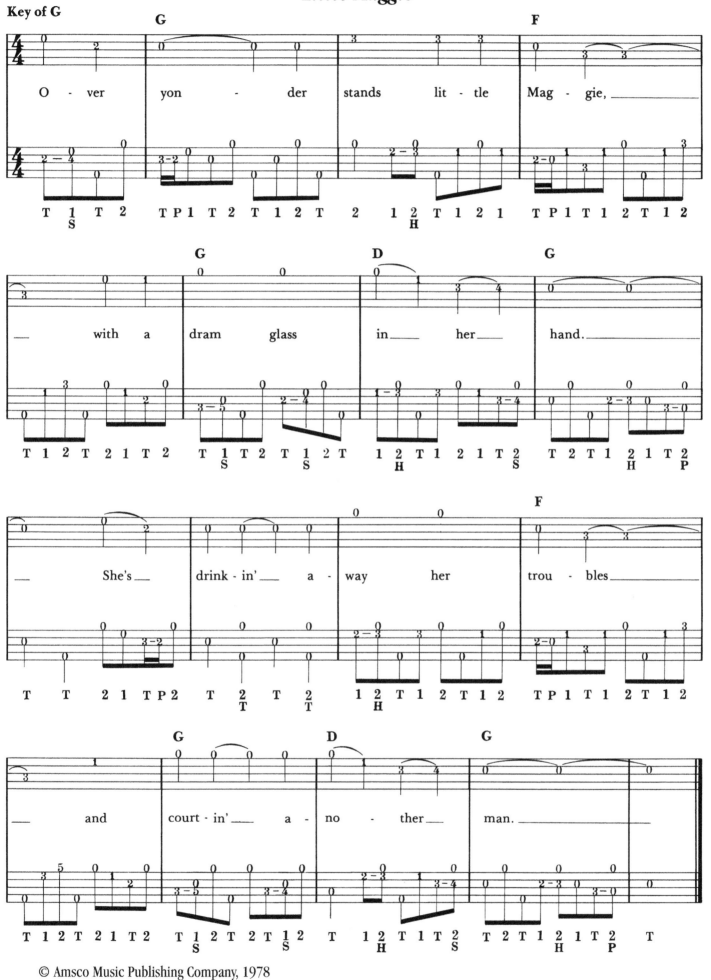

Will the Circle Be Unbroken

Capo on 2nd fret:
actual Key of D

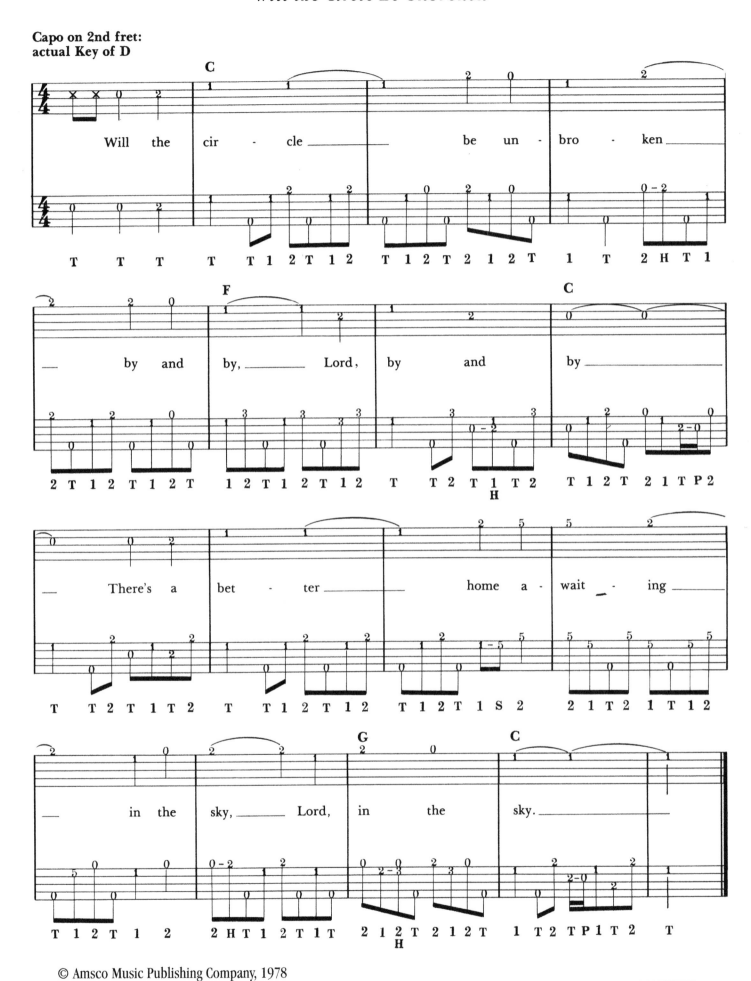

Pretty Polly

Capo on 2nd fret:
actual Key of A

Nine Pound Hammer

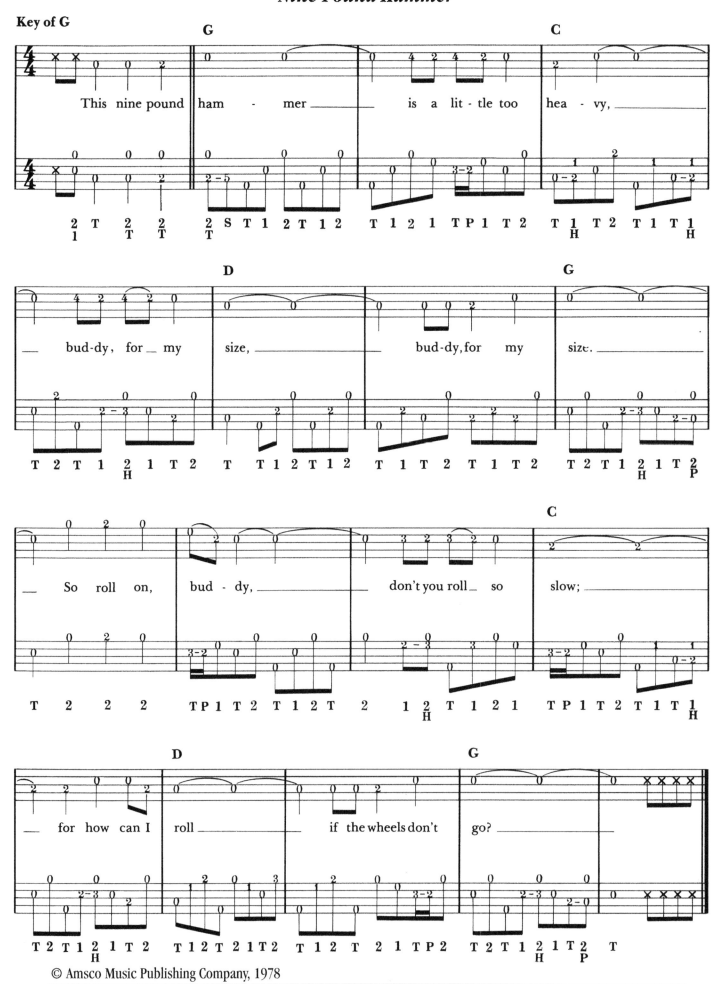

Reno Style

Earl Scruggs is the father of bluegrass banjo and his genius is not to be denied. But there was another man playing in a style very similar to Scruggs in the early forties—Don Reno. Bill Monroe was taken enough by Don's playing in 1943 to offer him a job with the Blue Grass Boys—this, a full two years before Earl. As luck would have it, though, Don was forced to hang up his fingerpicks and tour Burma with the army. When he returned, he picked up the banjo once again only to have people ask him where he learned to play like Scruggs. Understandably perturbed, Don went on to develop an entirely new jazzy banjo style. It was characterized, in large part, by a single string technique involving just the thumb and index finger of the right hand. This created a flatpicking effect that, for the first time in bluegrass, allowed the player to move beyond the chordally-oriented Scruggs licks into the realm of actual melody lines.

The following licks and exercises utilize this style and should give you an idea of Don's tremendous contribution to bluegrass banjo.

Now here's a Renofied version of *Wabash Cannonball* to show you just how these licks fit in.

Wabash Cannonball

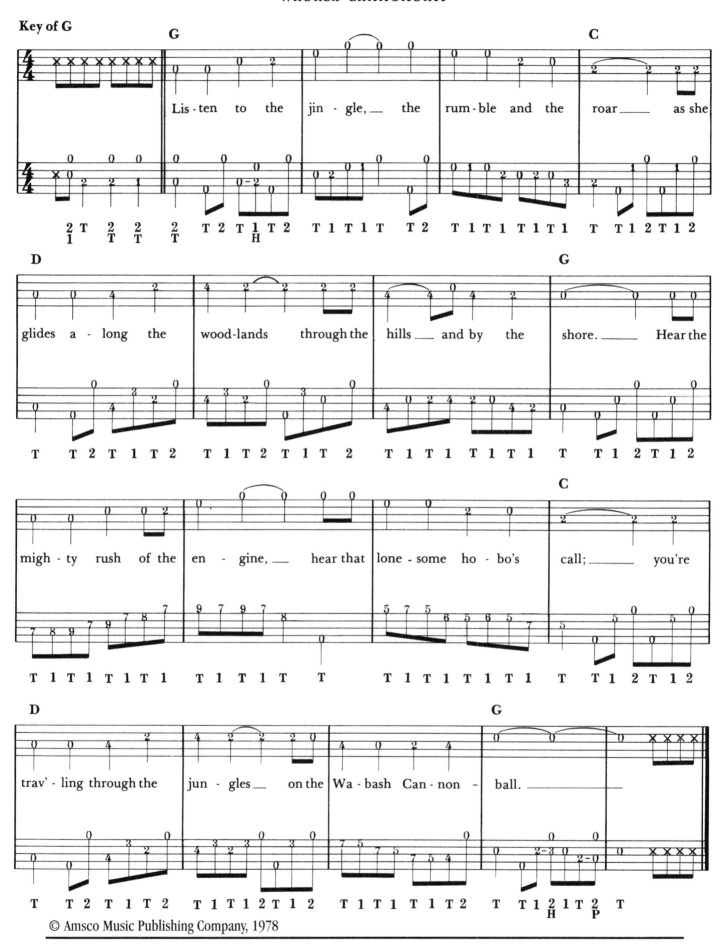

The Melodic Style

The melodic style is a relatively recent bluegrass technique. It was popularized in the early 1960s by Boston-born Bill Keith who decided that it was entirely possible to play fiddle tunes note for note on the banjo. His renditions of *Devil's Dream, Sailor's Hornpipe* and *Blackberry Blossom* demonstrated this and within a short time droves of northern-urban-middle-class banjo pickers were abandoning their Scruggs licks for the hot new scales and baroque acrobatics of the melodic (or "Keith") style. This posed a threat to the conservative bluegrass establishment that wanted the banjo mummified in a state of Scruggsification. As evolution would have it, however, progress marched on and today the melodic style is *the* other way to pick.

For all of its flashy techniques the melodic style is actually rather simple. Try this:

In those two tones you have the essence of the whole style—alternating strings (many of them open) to produce note-for-note melodies. The following G scale will give you a more graphic demonstration.

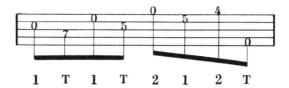

Just for comparison here's the same scale in Reno style:

Again, you can plainly see the melodic reliance on alternating strings to produce a smooth flowing sound. To get this alternation the focus is shifted from the first four or five frets—the site of most Scruggs licks—to the area between the fourth and seventh frets. The Reno style gets the same notes lower down the neck by doubling and quadrupling up on single strings. In the process it creates a more percussive sound. Notice, also, that the melodic style employs all three fingers of the right hand as opposed to just thumb and index for Reno. It's important to remember that this isn't a case of one style being better than the other. Rather, it's a question of taste. Each has its advantages. It is a fact that if you want to play a fiddle tune note for note from beginning to end, it's infinitely easier to use the melodic style. At the same time, there are many licks that are much more appropriate when rendered Renoically.

Now we're going to expand your grasp of melodic technique with the following exercises. In addition to preparing you for the rest of this section, many of these make nice licks in themselves.

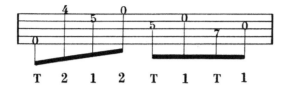

T 2 1 2 T 1 T 1

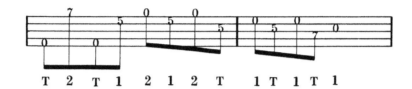

T 2 T 1 2 1 2 T   1 T 1 T 1

T 1 T 1 2 T 1 2   T 1 T 2 T

1 T 1 2 T 1 T 1   2 T 1 2 T 1 T 1   2 T 1 2 T 1 T 2   T

2 1 T 1 2 T 1 T   1

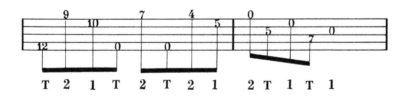

T 2 1 T 2 T 2 1   2 T 1 T 1

We're going to finish off now with six fiddle tunes. Although these are most obviously what the melodic style is all about, keep in mind the fact that melodies can be integrated into a Scruggs flow with fantastic results. So experiment on your own and see what you can come up with.

Capo on 2nd fret:
actual Key of A

Devil's Dream

Traditional
in the style of
Bill Keith

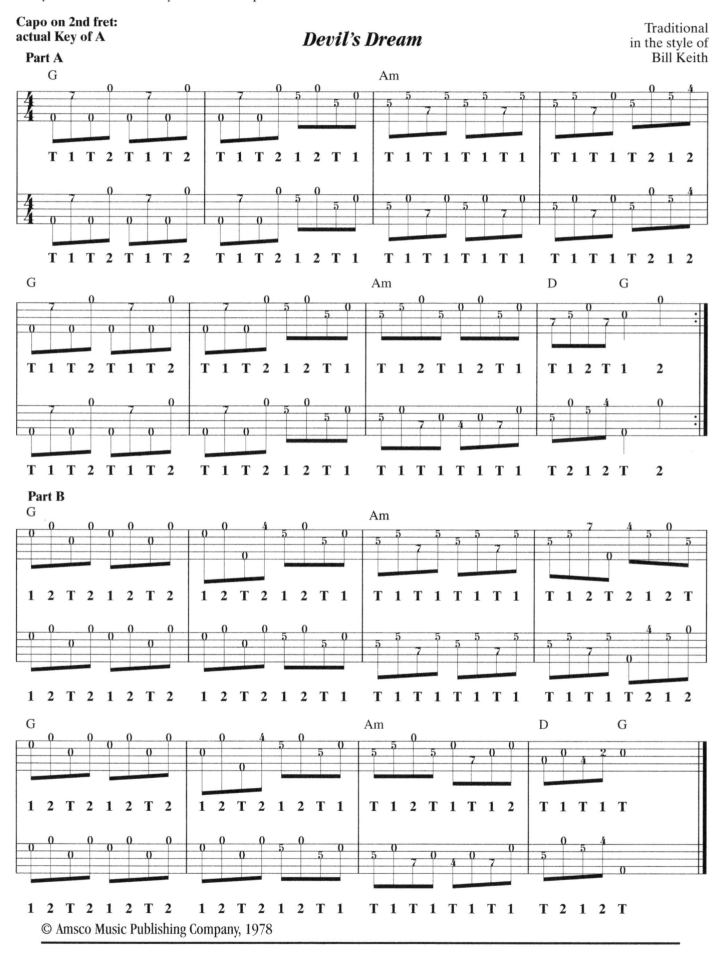

Arkansas Traveller

Key of D

Part A

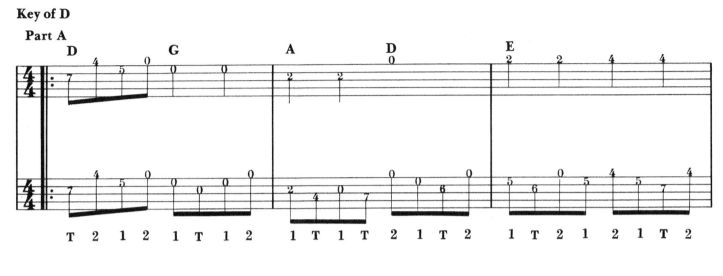

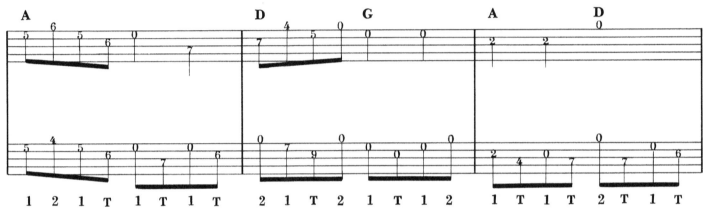

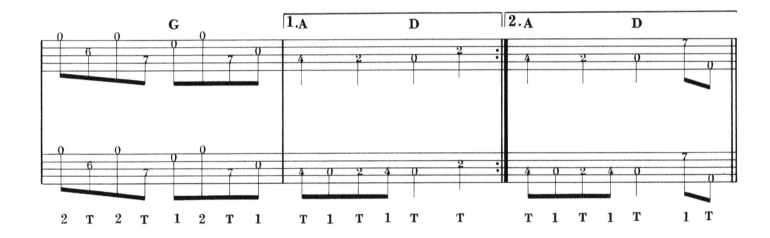

Part B

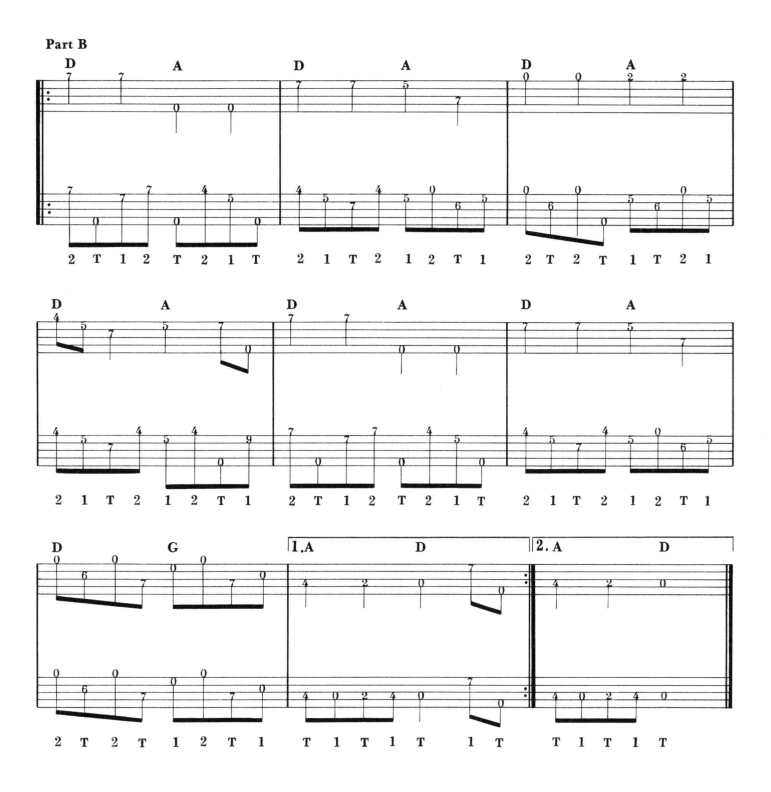

Blackberry Blossom

Key of G

Part A

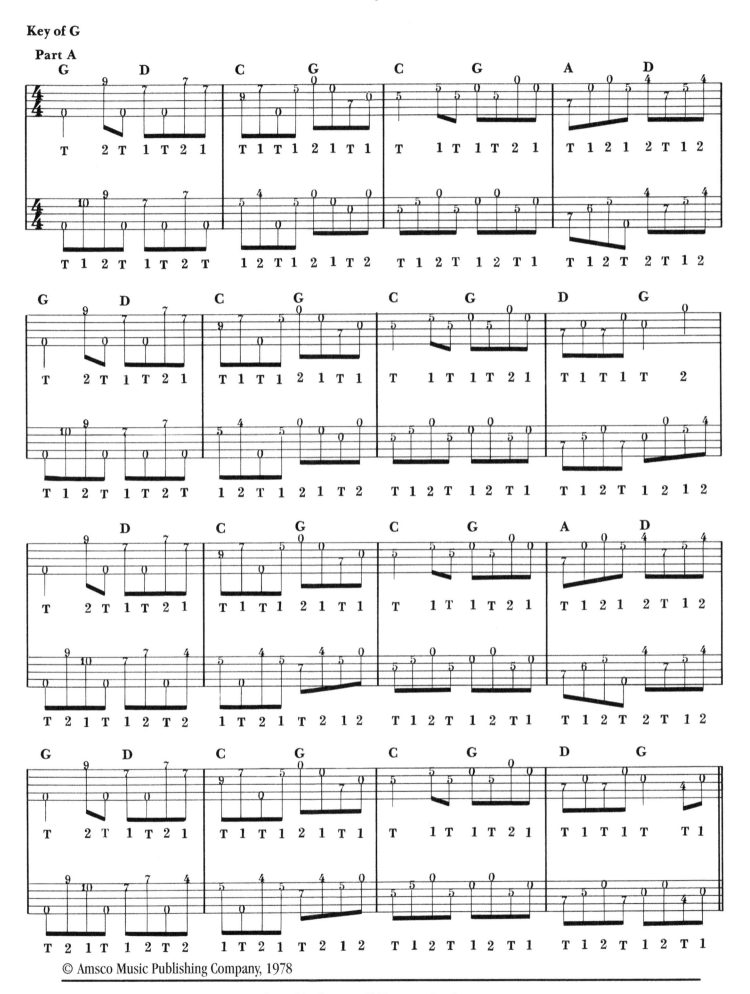

Part B

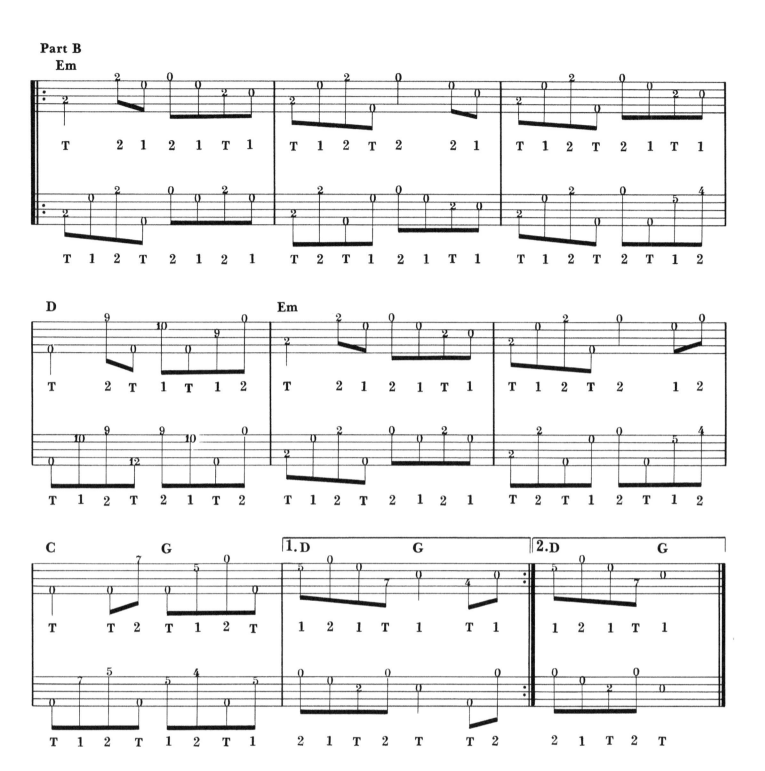

Turkey in the Straw

Key of G

Part A

Soldier's Joy

Backup

Even though it's as important as lead playing, backup is one of the more neglected aspects of bluegrass banjo. So in this next section I'm going to give you tips and tunes to get you started.

Earl Scruggs wrote the book on backup in the last forties and early fifties. But he didn't just rely on chunking off-beats (mandolin style). He also came up with a whole new framework of licks and roll combinations that added a jazzy punch and bounce to the music. His playing behind Lester Flatt in the early days is a masterful example of timing, finesse and sensitivity to the other musicians.

Sensitivity to the other musicians—that's the key to backup. Listen to what everyone else is doing, especially the person singing or playing the lead. If he or she leaves a short opening in his or her music, that's where you can fill in. The rest of the time you're there to provide solid support. And that means timing. If you can maintain a strong, even rhythm, that will create all sorts of space for the lead player to take off with his or her break. In addition, it will add to the overall tightness of the band. After all, the real joy in this (or any) music comes when you have a group of musicians cooking together effortlessly as one unit. Again, this is where the metronome comes in handy.

Also, you should pay attention to volume. Be careful not to overpower the lead. I know I've talked about getting a big sound out of your banjo, and there's a place for that. But you also have to know when to bring the volume down. If you listen to J.D. Crowe and the New South, you'll find that there's almost no playing going on during their vocal choruses, with the exception of fills. Go for contrast. Since you're usually going to be working with only three chords and a beat that doesn't change much from song to song, you'll need these dynamics to help keep things interesting. To do this, move your right hand away from the bridge (almost to the neck) for the quiet backup, and then get into your standard, hard driving Scruggs stance for the heavy-duty backup. Now that you know *how* to do it, I'll show you *where* to do it.

Here are a couple of general backup techniques that will work well behind medium to fast songs.

Although this first example is written in the key of C, it can be repeated anywhere on the neck (D at the 12th fret, G at the 17th fret, etc.). Use your thumb to fret the seventh fret of the fifth string.

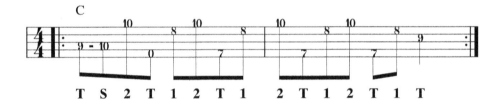

Notice, here, the extensive use of forward rolls, the most effective way to get a driving sound, up or down the neck.

This next short figure can also be repeated over and over again at different locations on the fretboard. The X at the bottom of the second quarter note means that you should lift your fingers ever so slightly off the fingerboard to create a damping effect.

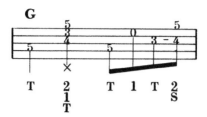

A variation of this lick can be found at the beginning of *Dark Hollow*.

To close things out, here's a backup lick that can be used effectively on slow songs. If you're worried about doubling your index finger on the first two notes, take heart. As I said, this is for slow songs. So you'll have plenty of time to play both notes without twisting your fingers into a pretzel.

When you're playing this lick concentrate on putting some bounce into it. That can really make things jump. For the prime example of bounce-oriented banjo, listen to Allen Shelton. (*Shelton's Special*—Rounder 0088). By the way, it wouldn't be such a bad idea to start incorporating that bounce into all of your playing. Keep it in mind.

O.K., that's a brief synopsis on backup. Even more than the lead, backup is best learned in conjunction with recordings or live music. There's just so much finesse involved here; you can't communicate it all via the printed page. So pick up some early Flatt and Scruggs recordings, play through these next four songs and you'll be on your way.

Salty Dog

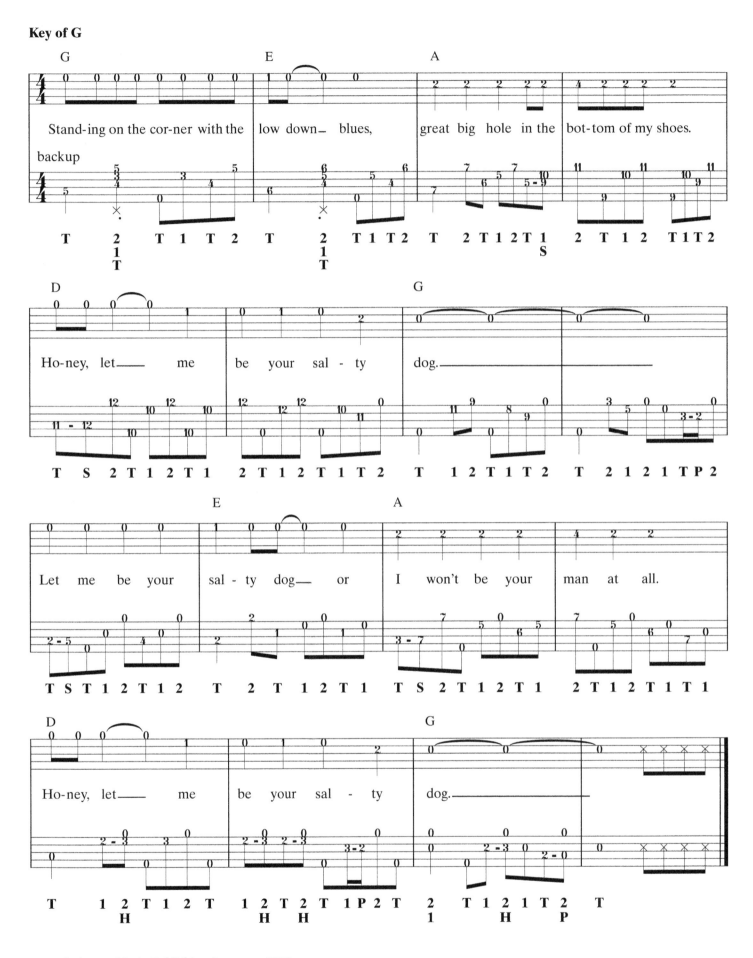

Salty Dog

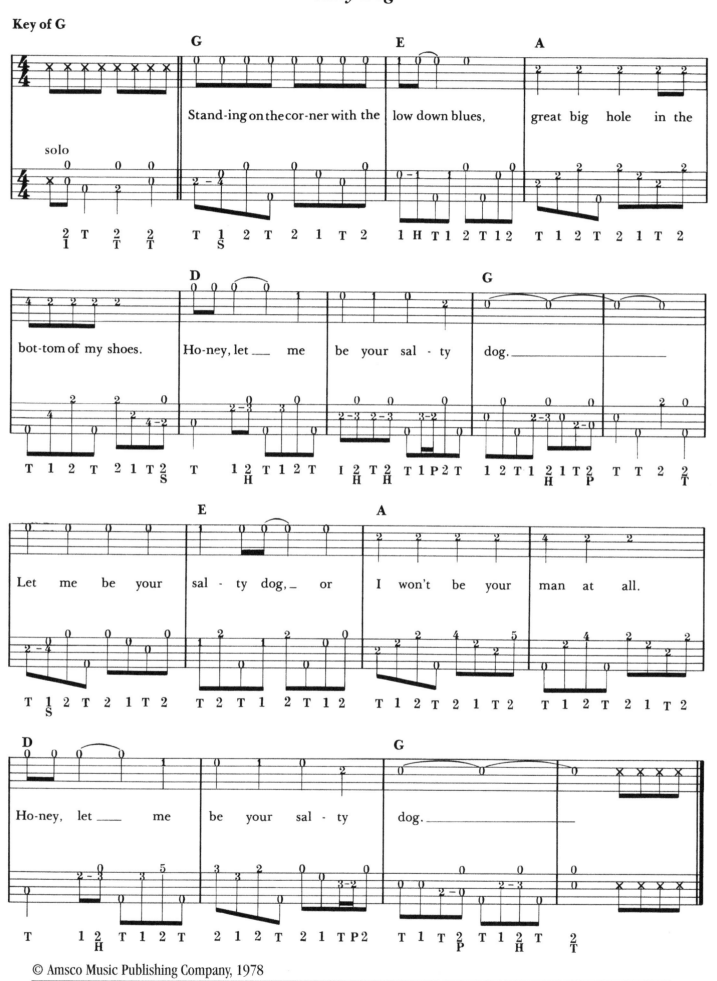

Sally Goodin

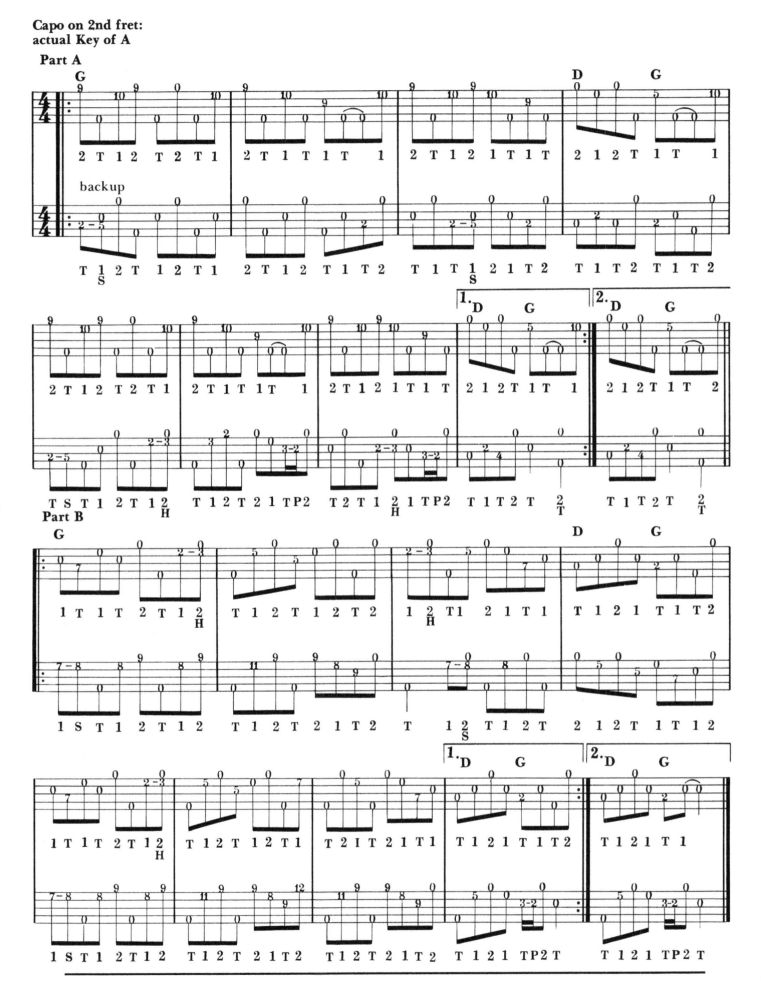

Sally Goodin

Part A

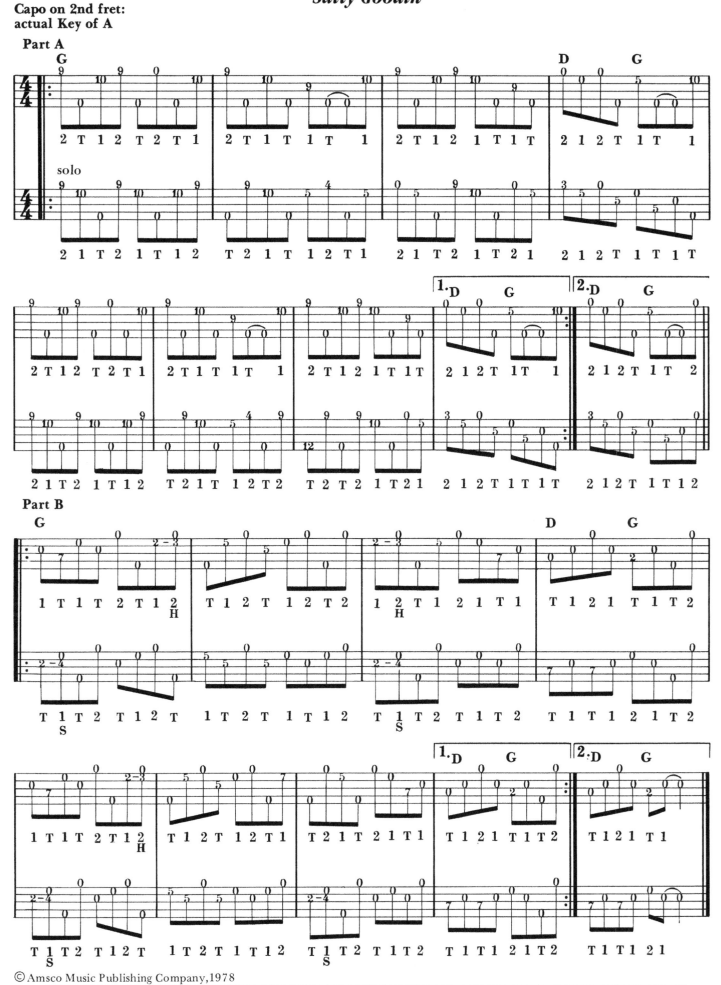

Part B

Dark Hollow

Capo on 2nd fret:
actual Key of D

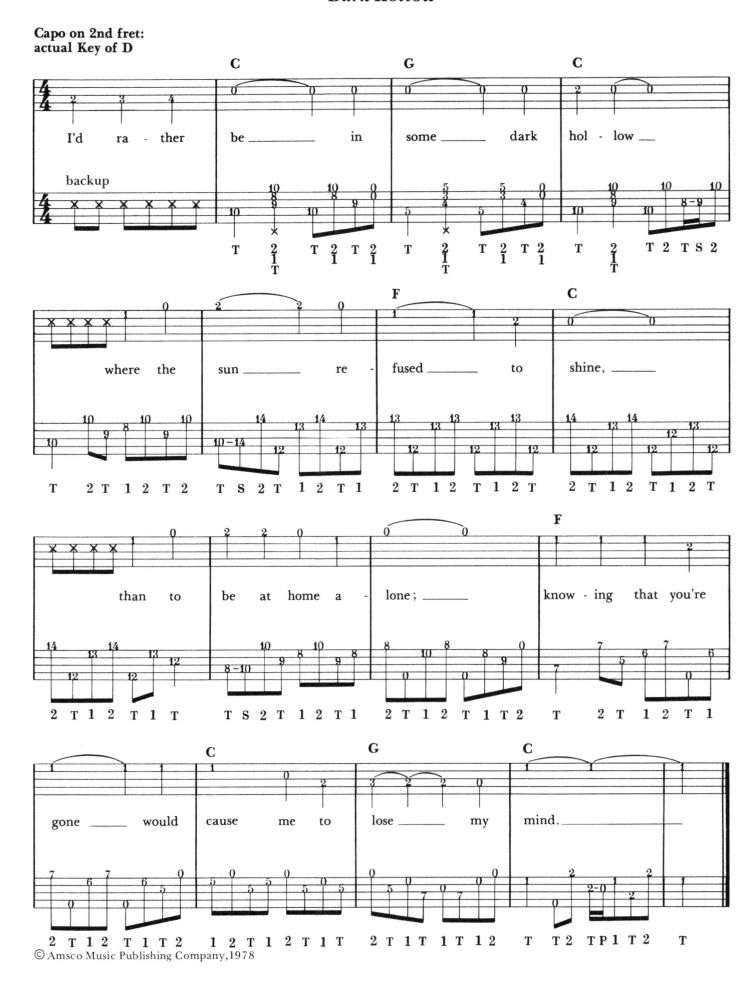

Dark Hollow

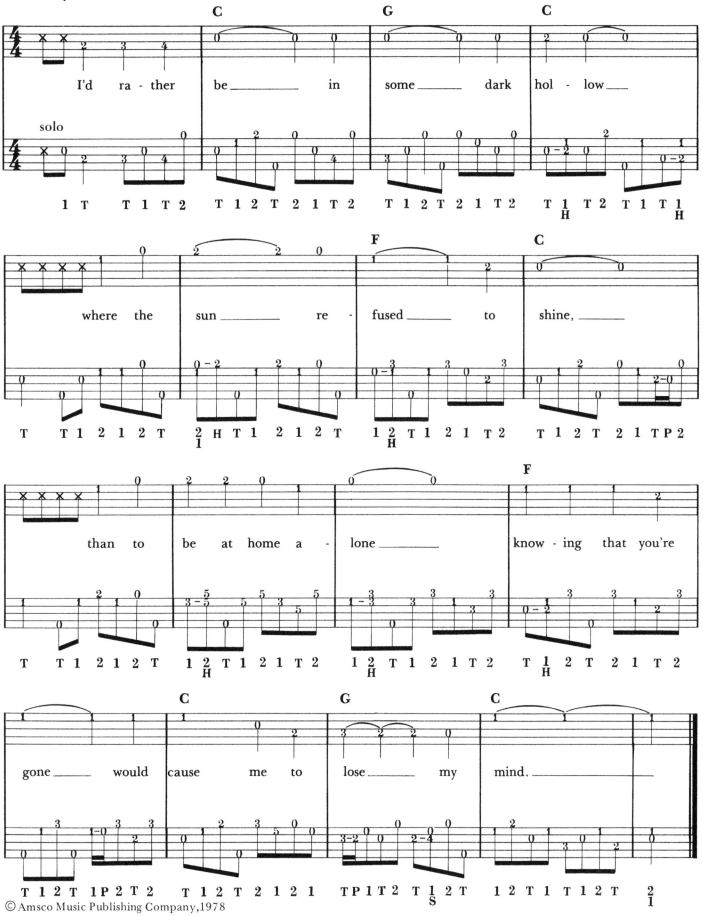

Other Tunings

Thus far, every song in the book has been in standard G tuning. This is because GDGBD gives us the open, hard driving sound necessary for pushing a bluegrass band. Indeed, that's why Scruggs used it almost exclusively when he was first showcasing his new style with Bill Monroe. And since his was the classic sound that every fledgling bluegrass banjo player sought to emulate, we find ourselves, today, playing primarily in G tuning.

This isn't to say you should avoid other tunings. *Au contraire.* The very first song that Earl worked out in the three-finger style was in D tuning—*Ruben's Train.*

D tuning is similar to G in that it gives you an open chord when you strum across the strings. Also, many of the Scruggs positions used in G tuning work just as well in D (as you'll see in *Ruben's Train*). Still, the D tuning has its own unique personality. To get into D, simply tune the fifth and third strings down a half step to F♯ and the second string down a whole step to A.

Other tunings are sometimes used when desired notes are too low to fall within the range of the G tuning. Such is the case with the C tuning, represented here by *Farewell Blues.* By taking your fourth string and tuning it down a whole step to C, you'll get a rich, low, bottomy sound that will keep you placid for hours.

In addition to the G, C, and D, there are many other tunings, each with their own distinct flavor, which can give you new insights into the potential of your instrument. Here are three more just to get you started.

full C: GCGCD

modal: GDGCD (see *Shady Grove*)

saw mill: F♯CGAD

Ruben's Train

Key of D
Tuning: F♯ D F♯ A D

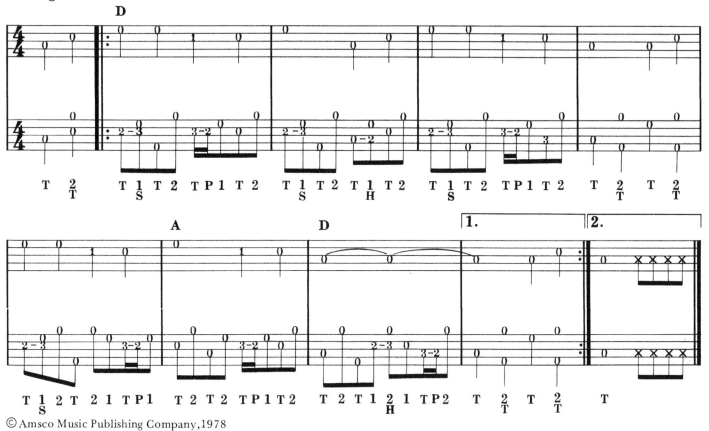

© Amsco Music Publishing Company, 1978

Shady Grove

Key of Gm
Tuning: G D G C D

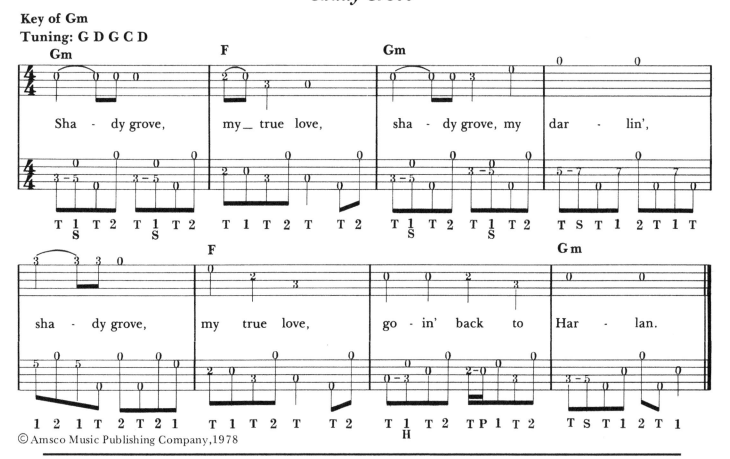

Sha - dy grove, my_ true love, sha - dy grove, my dar - lin',

sha - dy grove, my true love, go - in' back to Har - lan.

© Amsco Music Publishing Company, 1978

Farewell Blues

**Capo on 2nd fret:
actual Key of D**

Tuning: G C G B D

Rapollo, Pettis, Meyers, Schoebel

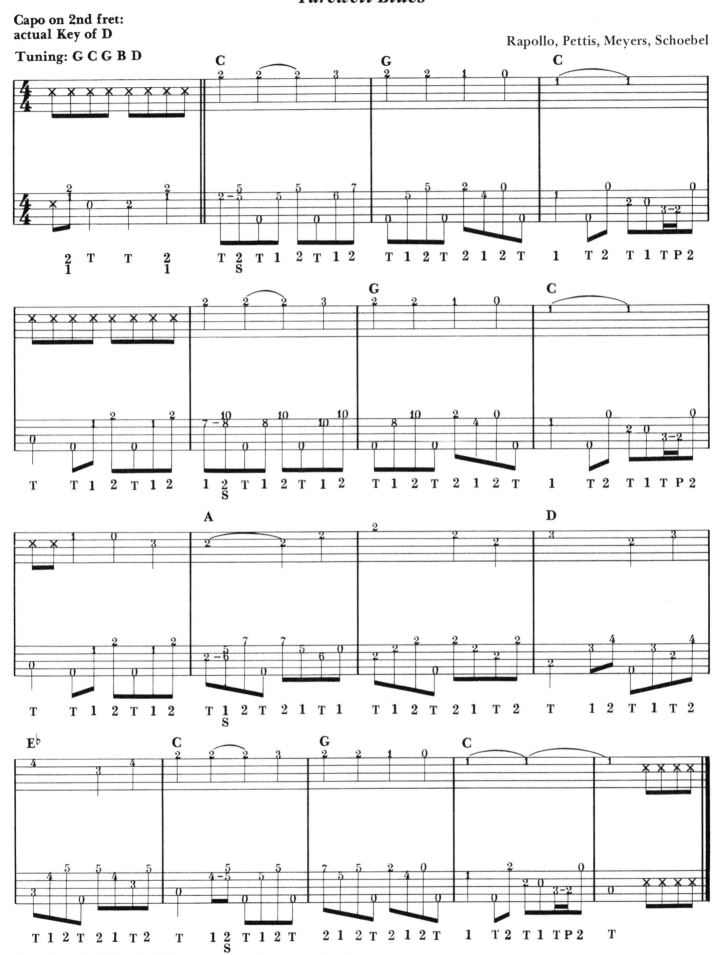

Improvising

Now that you're getting this music solidly implanted in your fingers, let's move from worked-out breaks to a bit of improvisation. Playing off the top of one's head is as important in bluegrass as it is in jazz, though bluegrass obviously orbits somewhat closer to earth. To ease your way into improvising, I want to talk about interchangeable licks.

If you'll remember back to the beginnings of the Scruggs, Reno and melodic sections, you learned a number of basic licks that fit nicely in a variety of settings. Those licks could just as easily have been replaced by an infinite number of substitute licks. And that's the secret of basic improvising. If you have a constantly expanding repertoire of interchangeable licks for every chord you might want to play, your music will always sound fresh. Since bluegrass banjo is primarily concerned with only three chords (The I, IV and V out of the G position), your job is an easy one.

What I'm going to do now is give you five licks each for the G, C and D chords. After that you'll have a chance to play through a version of *Bile 'Em Cabbage Down* that will incorporate a number of those licks to simulate an improvised break. Here they are.

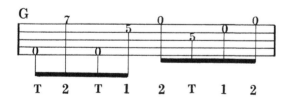

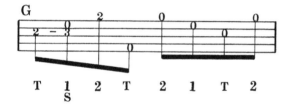

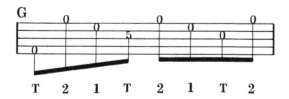

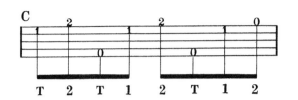

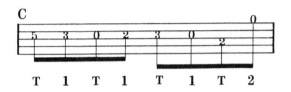

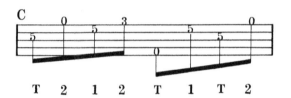

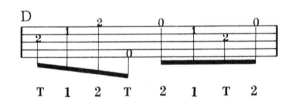

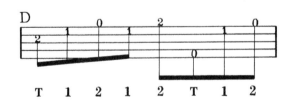

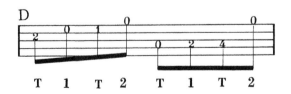

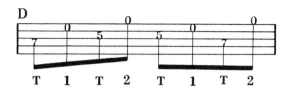

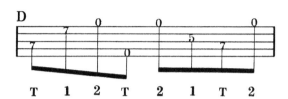

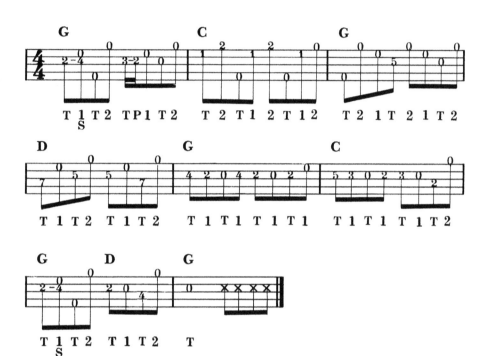

You can get a feel for real improvising by making your own substitutions for the chord changes above. Remember, any of the five G licks are playable against any of the G chords. The same holds true for the C and D licks. Note, however, that the last two measures should remain the same as they are in the example above. That means you'll have the first six measures to play with. This will ultimately lead you to the creation of original licks that will more fully express the creative aspects of your personality. And that's when you'll really start playing music.

Finale

This last section is a potpourri of songs intertwining Scruggs, Reno and melodic styles. Pay special attention to *Stoney Creek*. It's probably the most chordally involved tune in the book and as such points the way to the more advanced sounds to come. If you feel that you want to delve further into the intricacies of bluegrass banjo, consult the discography and bibliography for additional sources of input. Enjoy.

John Hardy

Key of G

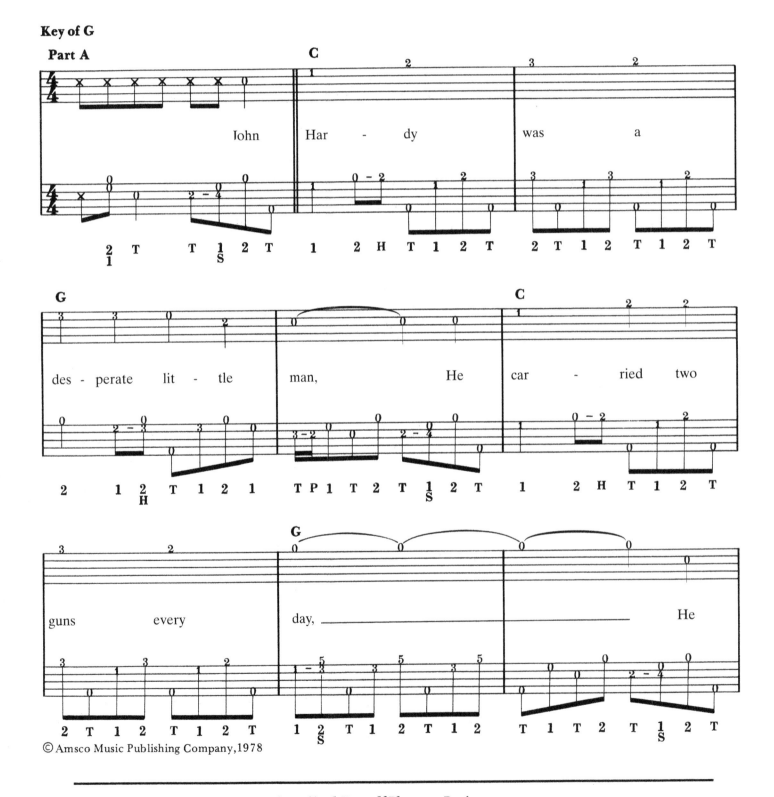

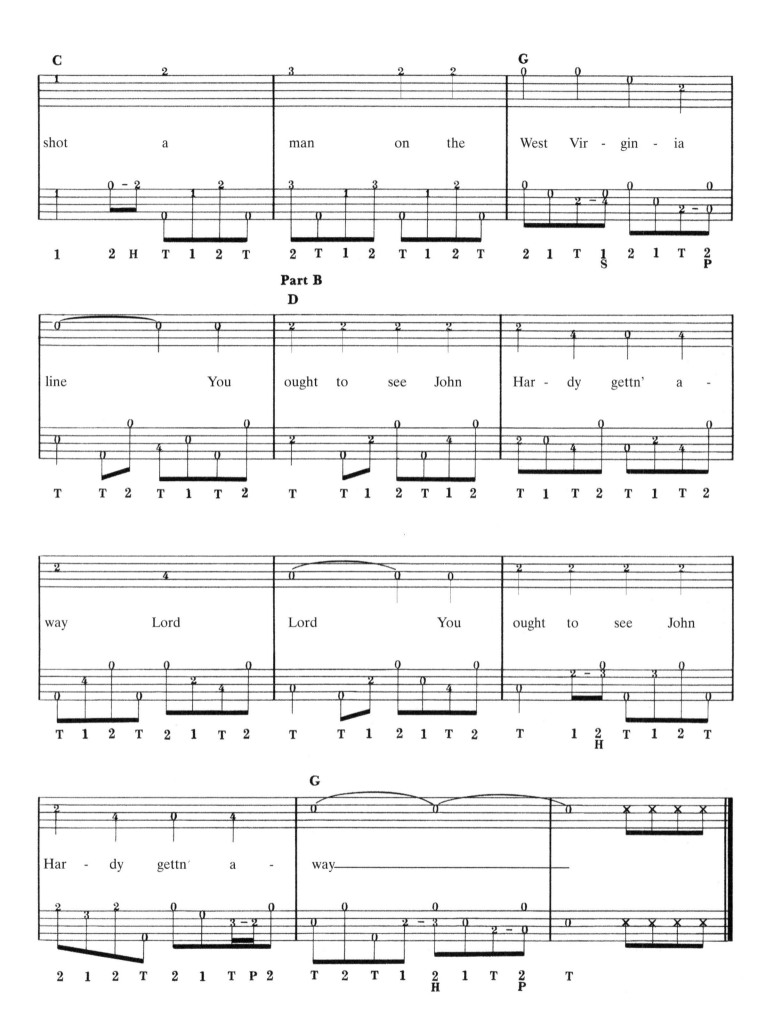

Sitting on Top of the World

Capo on 2nd fret:
actual Key of A

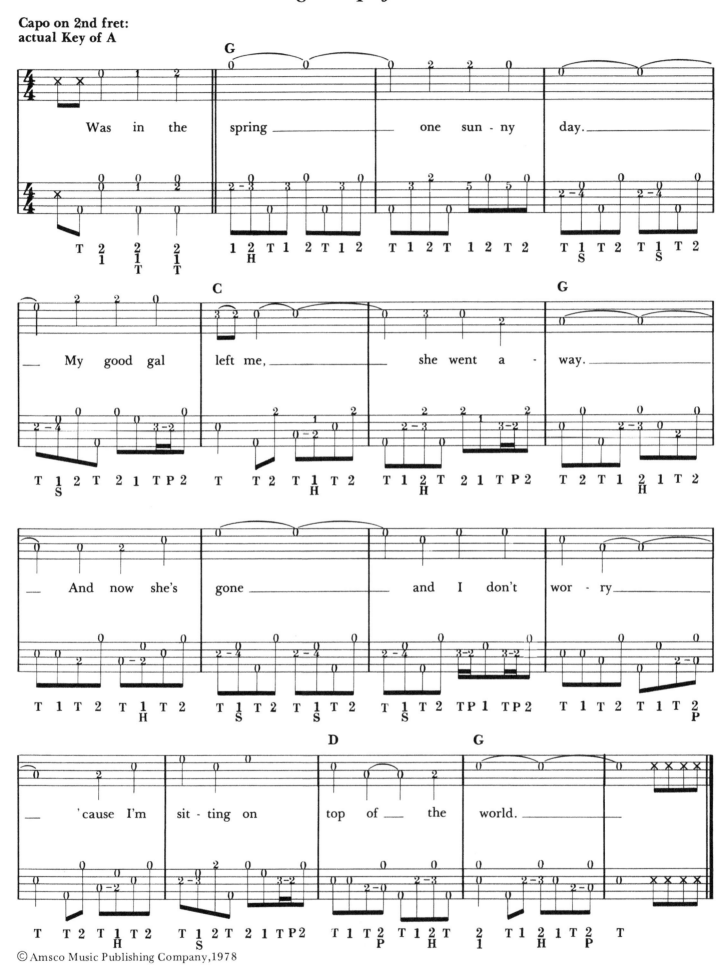

Was in the spring _____ one sun - ny day. _____

_____ My good gal left me, _____ she went a - way. _____

_____ And now she's gone _____ and I don't wor - ry _____

_____ 'cause I'm sit - ting on top of _____ the world. _____

Live and Let Live

Capo on 4th fret:
actual Key of B

Wiley Walker and Gene Sullivan

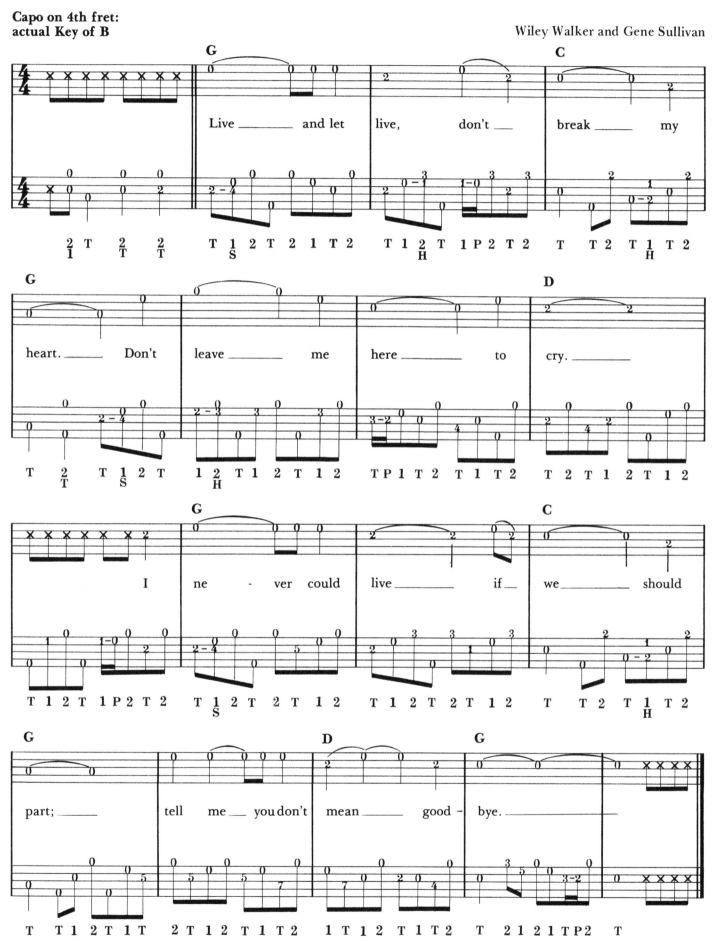

Bugle Call Rag

Key of G

Pettis, Meyers, Schoebel

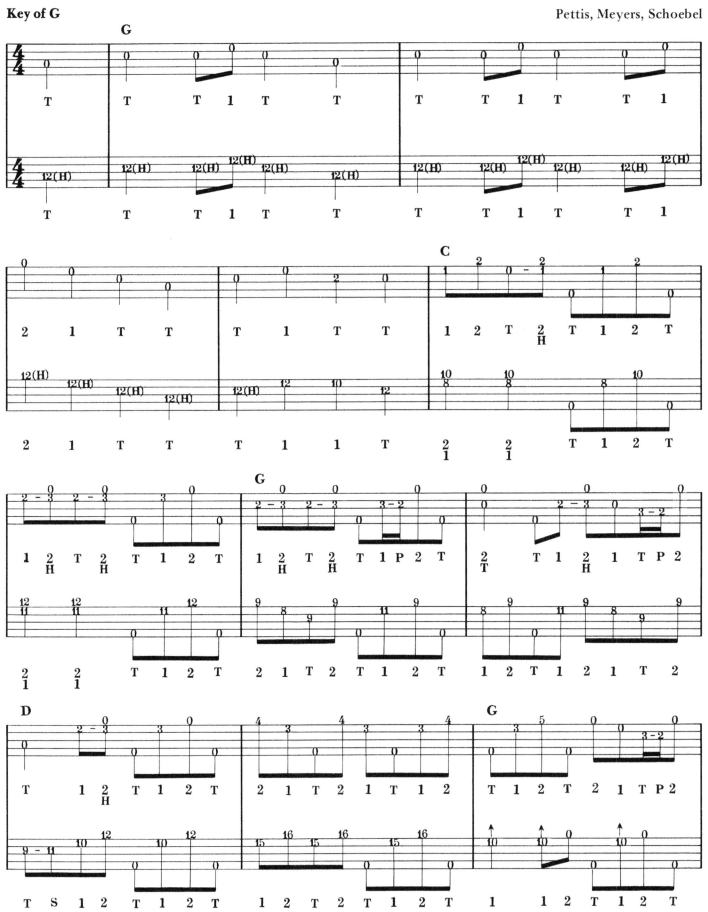

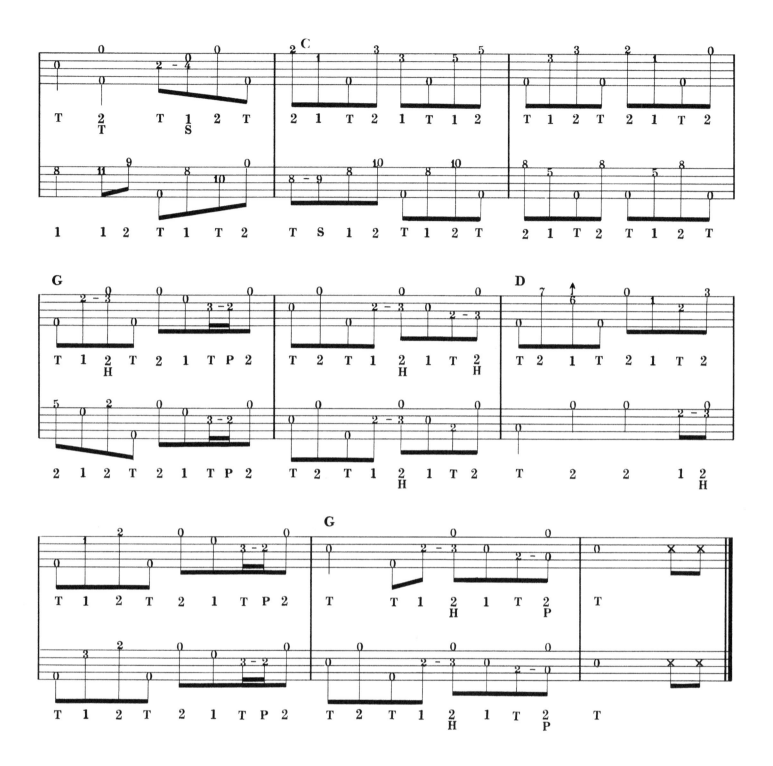

Stoney Creek

Capo on 2nd fret:
actual Key of A

Jesse McReynolds

Part A

Discography

Now that we're at the end of the book it's time to think of the subtleties of banjo playing that you just can't pick up from the printed page. And that's where recordings come in.

You see, you already have a particular way of playing some of the standard licks you've learned here. In addition, there are probably two or three other ways of approaching these licks that you may not have been aware of. For instance, J.D. Crowe probably plays them a little bit differently than you do, as does Earl Scruggs. Then there's the question of right-hand attack, Allen Shelton plays with a tremendous amount of bounce while Ralph Stanley uses a more straightforward right-hand approach. By listening to recordings you can become aware of some of these nuances and choose the ones you want to add depth to your own playing. There's also the sheer excitement and pleasure that comes from hearing a great banjo break on a CD (or live, for that matter) and that can do more for getting this music in your soul than one hundred pages of tablature.

Although bluegrass CDs are becoming more readily available in record stores these days you may still have trouble locating some of the out of the way labels. If this is the case you should write to the following mail order companies for their catalog. Service is quick and the selection is excellent:

County Sales
P.O. Box 191
Floyd, VA 24091

Sugar Hill
P.O. Box 55300
Durham, NC 27717-5300

Rounder Records
1 Camp St.
Cambridge, MA 02140
1-800 ROUNDER

Many of the CDs on the following list can be ordered from these companies. The list is a representative sampling of the best banjo recordings on the market today. If you can only afford three or four of these I suggest you stick to the tried and true—Scruggs, Reno or Osborne. These men represent the roots of this music. So listen to them first to find out where you're coming from. Then branch out from there.

Artists	Title	Label
Jimmy Arnold	*Southern Soul*	Rebel 1621
Eddie Adcock with The Country Gentlemen	*Folk Songs & Bluegrass*	Smithsonian Folkways CD-SF 40022
J.D. Crowe	*J.D. Crowe & The New South*	Rounder CD-0044
Vic Jordan	*Kenny Baker Plays Bill Monroe*	County 2708 CD

Courtney Johnson *with New Grass Revival*	*New Grass Revival*	Capitol 35161
Bill Keith	*Something Auld,* *Something Newgrass,* *Something Borrowed,* *Something Bluegrass*	Rounder 0084
Bill Knopf	*On Banjo*	First-CD006
Jimmy Martin *with J.D. Crowe*	*You Don't Know My Mind*	Rounder SS21
Jim Mills	*Bound to Ride*	Sugar Hill 3883
Alan Munde	*Blue Ridge Express*	Rounder 0301
The Osborne Brothers	*The Best of The Osborne Brothers*	Sugar Hill 2203
Reno & Smiley	*On Stage*	Copper Creek 127
Earl Scruggs	*Blue Ridge Cabin Home*	Rebel 102
Allen Shelton	*Shelton Special*	Rounder 0088
Ralph Stanley	*Bound to Ride*	Rebel 1114
Don Stover	*Things in Life*	Rounder 0014
Tony Trischka	*The Early Years*	Rounder 11578
Eric Weissberg	*with Pete Seeger* *and Roger McGuinn* *Banjo Jamboree: Traditional Series*	Rykodisc 1019
Peter Wernick *with Country Cooking*	*Country Cooking:* *26 Instrumentals*	Rounder 11551

Magazines

If you're feeling rich you can subscribe to both of the following major bluegrass magazines:

Bluegrass Unlimited
Box 111
Broad Run, VA 22014

Banjo Newsletter
P.O. Box 3418
Annapolis, MD 21403-0418

I especially recommend the *Banjo Newsletter* because it concentrates solely on the banjo. Every month it contains informative articles, interviews, tablature, and tips on playing. It's worth it for the inspirational value alone.

At Fox Hollow, New York

Bibliography

This book has been an hors d'oeuvre—a taste of bluegrass banjo. If it has satisfied your appetite, I am pleased. However, if you still desire the main course, I suggest you choose from the following menu. *Bon appetit.*

Bluegrass Banjo by Peter Wernick (Oak Publications)—This book ranges from beginning to advanced instruction with attention to all details in-between. Highly recommended.

Earl Scruggs and the Five String Banjo by Earl Scruggs (Peer)—Here Earl has provided us with a generous sampling of his tunes and breaks, written out as he originally played them. Everyone should buy this.

Banjo Songbook by Tony Trischka (Oak)—Over seventy-five songs in tablature, featuring bluegrass, fiddle tunes, and classical compositions. Plus, a bonus history of the three-finger style of playing. This is an excellent way to beef up your repertoire.

Melodic Banjo by Tony Trischka (Oak)—A complete guide to the melodic style featuring interviews with and the music of Bill Keith, Bobby Thompson, Alan Munde, et al.

Hot Licks and Fiddle Tunes for the Bluegrass Banjo by Bill Knopf (Chappell Music)—Bill is a fine West Coast player who has collected some of his favorite scales, licks and endings and put them into this book. With the addition of twelve fiddle tunes at the end, this makes a great way to spice up your playing.

5-String Banjo Fiddle Tunes (Mel Bay)—An explanation and a collection of songs in the melodic style. More choice tunes for your repertoire.